W9-COY-398

I'm Glad I'm Me

Weaving the Thread of Love from Generation to Generation

To Libby and Lexie,
I'm Glad you are you
Sheila Aron

By Sheila Aron

Illustrated by Charlotte Arnold

EAKIN PRESS Waco, Texas

FIRST EDITION
Copyright © 2008
By Sheila Aron
Published in the United States of America
By Eakin Press
A Division of Sunbelt Media, Inc.
P.O. Box 21235 - Waco, Texas 76702
email: sales@eakinpress.com
: website: www.eakinpress.com :
ALL RIGHTS RESERVED.

1 2 3 4 5 6 7 8 9
EAN 978-1-934645-37-6
ISBN 1-934645-37-0

Dedication

In loving memory of my son Matthew.

To my parents, Lena and Leon.

—Sheila Aron

For my beloved mother Gloria who lived to see her fourth generation

and to Donovan and Lorna who were inspirations for the illustrations.

—Charlotte Arnold

Love, like a thread, weaves and entwines.
    Love leaves memories that last throughout time.

Love can be shared anytime anywhere,
    Love is being there—showing that you care.

Love is the key to be all you can be,
    Love makes you think **"I'm glad I'm me."**

Love can be shared when you wake up in the morning.

Good morning, **I love you**.
You always make me feel happy.
When I'm with you...**I'm glad I'm me.**

...when you have done your best.

I admire you for trying.
You gave your all and that is one
of many   reasons why **I love you**.

...when you are sad.

Can I help?

When I feel sad I talk to someone I trust.

I love you and I am here whenever
you need me.

...when you have been helpful.

How thoughtful of you.
Your acts of kindness make me
love you even more.

...when you are shy.

I understand. There are times when I feel shy, too. **I love you** as you are. I'm glad you're you and

I'm glad I'm me.

. . . when you are having fun.

I love the sweet sound of your laughter.

Because of you. . .

I'm glad I'm me.

Our love helps us to be strong.

Together we can face our fears...

...when you are afraid.

...when you need a friend.

You are everything a friend should be
—kind, considerate, loving and fun.
I _love you_ and treasure your friendship.
With you beside me...

...when you go to school.

Listen, ask, learn and laugh.

Enjoy your day and remember

that **I love you** very much.

... when you disagree.

Let's talk and try to understand
how the other feels.
Talking about our problem
helps us work things out.

Even when we disagree, *I love you*.

...when we are working together.

Thank you for helping me.
Working or playing—
I *love* to be with **you**.

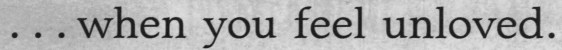

...when you feel unloved.

Love is for everyone, especially you.
Loving yourself is where love begins
and **I love you** too.

How do you show love to yourself?
By saying **"I'm glad I'm me."**

...when it is time to say "good bye."

Whether we are together or apart

I love you.

You are forever in my heart and thoughts.

When I think of you...

I'm glad I'm me.

...when you have been spoken to in a mean voice.

I am sorry for yelling at you.

Please forgive me.

Sometimes the way we say words can be hurtful.
I still **love you** and always will.

...when you are proud.

You did it! I knew that you could.

I love you and am proud of you

today and everyday.

...when your day is done.

Let's talk about all that you did today.
I love you,
That is why everything you do
is important to me.

...when it is time for bed.

Sweet dreams.
*Good night, **I love you**.*

I love you too.

"I'm glad I'm me."

Weave the thread of love
from generation to generation.

What is love?

How does being loved make you feel?

Who makes you feel loved?

How do you share your love?

What do you say to someone you love?

How have you been helpful lately? How did being helpful make you feel?

What words of love do you say to yourself?

Author photo by Zach Tate.

Sheila Aron was inspired to write this book for those who missed hearing the words "I love you" as a child. *I'm Glad I'm Me* teaches parents how easy it is to say "I love you" to their children. She is providing her book to families involved with the Children' Protective Service in Harris, County, Houston, Texas, ESCAPE Family Resource Center, Houston, Texas, and ChildBuilders, Houston, Texas.

Charlotte Arnold is a professional artist/illustrator working in Chicago.
Among her accomplishments is the painting "Forever Children" which she created as a fundraiser for the Emerald Coast Children' Advocacy Center in Florida. She makes her home in Naperville, Illinois, with her husband Bo.